Why Not a WOMAN?

McDougal & Associates

Servants of Christ and Stewards of the Mysteries of God

Why Not a WOMAN?

by

Vivian Collins

All Bible references are from the *Holy Bible,
King James Version,* public domain.

Published by:

McDougal & Associates
18896 Greenwell Springs Road
Greenwell Springs, Louisiana 70739
www.ThePublishedWord.com

McDougal & Associates is an organization dedicated to the
spreading of the Gospel of Jesus Christ to as many people as
possible in the shortest time possible.

ISBN 978-1-940461-86-1

Printed on demand in the US, the UK, and Australia
For Worldwide Distribution

Dedication

To the memory of my late husband, **Courtney George**

To my precious daughter, **Leticia Collins**

To my precious sister, **Dorisett Thornton,** who I love dearly and raised as a daughter. She lived with me until she graduated from college, married and moved to Georgia.

Acknowledgments

I would like to give thanks to Almighty God who lives on the inside of me and is increasing me daily. He Who daily encourages me is the same Who fearfully and wonderfully made me in the first place. It was He who spoke to me and said, "Why not, Vivian?" He said to me, "I knew you before you were conceived in your mother's womb," and He also said, "I know you by name, and you are Mine."

I want to honor my husband who has gone on to be with the Lord. He was my Sweetie, and he stood beside me in whatever the Holy Spirit inspired me to do. He was always by my side to encourage me in whatever I needed.

Thanks to Pastor and Prophetess Lolitha Pippins who was led to conduct a women's conference with the theme "WHY NOT A WOMAN?" It was that theme that touched me and inspired me to write this book,

My thanks to Pastor Patrick Adobe of Ghana, West Africa, who was a great inspiration to me and encouraged me to go forth.

I thank God for Janice Williams who said, "Write."

I thank God for Pastor Father G. Amaldoss, who also said, "Write!"

I thank God for Apostle Reginald Wilson who encouraged me and guided me to his publisher.

I pray God's blessing on each of their lives. May His blessings overtake them.

Of a truth I perceive that God is no respecter of persons.
Acts 10:34

Contents

POEMS

About the Cover

I searched through many pages of images concerning women before I found just the one I wanted to be the cover of this book. It is a very unusual shot, I'm sure you will agree, showing the hands of God (made up by many different people) holding a baby (again made up by many people). And it was taken from high above the crowd.

To me, this photo depicts exactly what I am trying to say in this book. God has us in His oh-so-capable hands, and therefore we have nothing to fear. His plan for us is a wonderful one, a plan which we each need to discover and follow, for He always knows best.

Vivian Collins

Introduction

This book was not intended to make women think they are better than men or to promote the Women's Liberation Movement. Rather it is to let women know that God has a plan for their lives. He created men and women equal and set the woman to walk alongside of her husband.

God has great expectations for your life. You are for far more than bearing children or being a good housewife. That is all good and be respected. I myself am the mother of three, and I count that an awesome privilege. But ask God if there might be something else He expects of you. Are there places you need to be going or things you need to be doing?

We must all be about our Father's business. For thee past thirteen years, I have had the privilege to travel to many mission field to speak God's Word, and I want to do it more. I went out because I heard God speak to me from His Word and say, "GO!"

God tells us to seek His face daily, and as we seek Him, He reveals Himself to us. He speaks to us, He leads us and guides us and takes us into deeper realms so that we can know the where, the what and the how of whatever it is He is calling us to do.

This requires that we be very prayerful, and it requires that our mates be in agreement. Everything that we do for God must be done in order. The prophet Amos declared:

Can two walk together, except they be agreed? Amos 3:3

The wise King Solomon wrote:

Two are better than one; because they have a good reward for their labour. For if they fall, the one will lift up his fellow: but woe to him that is alone when he falleth; for he hath not another to help him up. Ecclesiastes 4:9-10

Through the years, it has been proven that women can successfully do many things in life. We have great women doctors, teachers, lawyers, politicians, athletes and ministers. And yet some women still remain timid and allow fears to hold them back. I was one of those. But that was then, and this is now. Now I can boldly ask the questions:

WHY NOT A WOMAN? AND WHY NOT YOU?

Vivian Collins
Marrero, Louisiana

Chapter 1

Why Not A Woman?

Then Peter opened his mouth, and said, Of a truth I perceive that God is no respecter of persons: but in every nation he that feareth him, and worketh righteousness, is accepted with him.
Acts 10:34-35

I was privileged to attend a women's conference years ago that used the theme: "WHY NOT A WOMAN?" That theme spoke to me. The Spirit of God immediately spoke to my spirit and said, "WHY NOT A WOMAN?"

Then another question came to me, "Why not me?" Was there anything wrong with me? No, I came to realize. I knew my purpose, I knew who I was, and I knew Whose I was. For many years I had been teaching women classes on being strong in the Lord, not giving up, keeping the faith and what God would do for them as a result. Surely, God is no respecter of persons.

Why Not a Woman?

Years ago now God gave me a ministry to help hurting women, women going through hard times, women with children in prison, women with children on drugs or children slain in the streets. At the time, things were not as bad as they are now. Today this ministry is needed more than ever before.

My heart went out to women who were broken, and I had to let them know that they could rise again. They could get up from where they were and soar once again.

I invited women to my home, and we would sit around my dining room table, as I taught and encouraged them in the Word of God. My heart went out to women whose sons were being put to death. As a mother, that woman had carried her child for nine months and then given birth to him with such expectancy for the future. Now that he was being put to death, few could understand how she felt, how she hurt. That is a terrible feeling!

My heart melted inside of me. We are commanded in the Scriptures to weep with those who weep, and the compassion of Jesus within us makes this a reality:

Why Not A Woman?

Rejoice with them that do rejoice, and weep with them that weep.　　　Romans 12:15

We are also commanded to pray for one another:

Confess your faults one to another, and pray one for another, that ye may be healed. The effectual fervent prayer of a righteous man availeth much.　　　James 5:16

I told my pastor what God had put on my heart, and he allowed me to go on his television show and talk about this ministry. The result was that other women began to come and pour out their hearts to us. Today, I still have a radio program on the Internet dedicated to this ministry to hurting women.

A few years after we started this, some men wanted to come too. I asked God about it, and He said that His help was for all hurting people everywhere, not just women, so I opened my home to hurting men as well. These days there are so many hurting people in our world that I sense the need to speak with them one-on-

one. They need someone to hear their heart, someone who can relate to what they are feeling and saying, someone they can confide in. I qualify on all counts:

- I can tell you how my family went through a hard ordeal in marriage.
- I can tell you how I felt when I lost my mother at an early age. She was only forty-five and left behind eight children.
- I can tell you how I won my father and then lost him again.
- I can tell you how I lost my sister at the age of twenty-one.
- I can tell you how I went through a divorce.
- I can tell you how I suffered through the loss of a husband at the tender age of twenty-nine.
- I can tell you how I was tempted with cocaine by my uncle and was able to walk away free.
- I can tell you how I was tempted with alcohol with friends and had to take a stand and say no.

- I can tell you what it was like to have my eighteen-year-old son go to prison for murder.
- I can tell you what it was like to have a brother very close to me who became a crack addict.
- I can tell you what it felt like, after being married for just three years, for someone to call me and say, "Your husband is dead."
- I can tell you what it was like to be alone.

And, of course, there is more. When I lost my husband, I had three small children to provide for, and I lost it for the next six months. Tears ran down my face in the dark hours when there was no one to help me. But I didn't give up on God, and I didn't give up on fellowshipping with the believers.

What I am trying to say is that there are down lows and high times in life. It is what you make of it all that counts. Don't let anyone or anything steal your joy. Find time to laugh and be happy.

Paul said in Romans 7:15, *"For that I do I allow not; for what I would, that do I not; but what*

I hate, that do I." Never think that life is too hard for you. Someone else is going through the same thing or something worse and feels the same way you do. God has said:

> *To every thing there is a season, and a time to every purpose under the heaven.*
> Ecclesiastes 3:1

He didn't say that only the good things in life have a purpose. He said that *everything* has a purpose, and it is all guided by our Father in Heaven.

Why not a woman? God doesn't have a problem blessing us women. So why should you be limited?

WHY NOT A WOMAN?
AND WHY NOT YOU?

Chapter 2

Why Not You?

Wherefore seeing we also are compassed about with so great a cloud of witnesses, let us lay aside every weight, and the sin which doth so easily beset us, and let us run with patience the race that is set before us, looking unto Jesus the author and finisher of our faith; who for the joy that was set before him endured the cross, despising the shame, and is set down at the right hand of the throne of God.

Hebrews 12:1-2

Why not a woman? And why not you? God thought enough of you to make you a woman. So, why not you? God knew exactly the purpose He made you for and declared that you are highly favored. That's where love shows itself mighty, for we serve a mighty God.

Think about Mary, how she had to endure the hardships of her Son being beaten, had to watch Him being hung on a cross, had to listen to the beat of a hammer pounding nails into His hands and feet. Could you have withstood that? Mary did.

And yet there is an even greater grace available to us now. Jesus died for you and me, so that we may be strengthened to endure any and every hardship. Just as He sacrificed for us, can we not go forth, laying aside every weight, to run this race with dignity.

You and I have a race that is set before us. Let us run, not knowing exactly what is ahead but knowing *Who* is ahead.

I know that you are fearful, but why? He said:

"Fear not!"

This phrase is used seventy-one times in the King James Version of the Bible.

God said:

Fear not, little flock; for it is your Father's good pleasure to give you the kingdom. Luke 12:32

22

Why Not You?

God said through Paul:

For God hath not given us the spirit of fear; but of power, and of love, and of a sound mind. 2 Timothy 1:7

Whenever I feel a little fearful, I turn to the Word of God for comfort. God knew we were going to have some challenging times in our lives, and that is why His Word is there, to comfort us and bring us peace.

Yes, I realize that the devil will come to torment me with whatever I happen to be facing at the moment. There are many things that can bring on fear. It could be nothing more than a test of your faith and your confidence in knowing who is really living on the inside of you.

Jesus said,

Let you light so shine before men, that they may see your good works, and glorify your father which is in heaven. Matthew 5:16

After I lost my son to prison walls, many people came to me and said, "Vivian, I don't know how you held up under that, and I don't know what I would have done in the same situation, but I have watched how you walked through this and it inspired me."

Did I hurt? Oh, yes, I did! Did I become fearful? Absolutely, yes, I did! But, at the same time, I knew Who I had with me. When I felt like crying, I laughed in the midst of my hurt and pain. I stayed in church in the midst of my heartache and disappointment. I clung to Bible studies even though I was struggling myself. I did not separate myself from fellowshipping with fellow believers.

Do you know why you were created? God's Word declares:

But now thus saith the Lord that created thee, O Jacob, and he that formed thee, O Israel, Fear not: for I have redeemed thee, I have called thee by thy name; thou art mine. When thou passest through the waters, I will be with thee; and through the rivers, they shall not overflow thee: when thou walkest through the fire, thou shalt not be burned; neither shall the flame kindle upon thee. For I am the Lord thy God,

Why Not You?

the Holy One of Israel, thy Saviour: I gave Egypt for thy ransom, Ethiopia and Seba for thee. Since thou wast precious in my sight, thou hast been honourable, and I have loved thee: therefore will I give men for thee, and people for thy life. Fear not: for I am with thee: I will bring thy seed from the east, and gather thee from the west; I will say to the north, Give up; and to the south, Keep not back: bring my sons from far, and my daughters from the ends of the earth; even every one that is called by my name: for I have created him for my glory, I have formed him; yea, I have made him.

Isaiah 43:1-7

With that, allow me to tell you a little about my son. His name is Bernis Tyrell Brown, and he was eighteen at the time of his arrest. He was sentenced to prison for life, but he is now serving God and helping others. When he was arrested and charged with murder, there was a terrible war going on in my mind between the spirit and the devil. The devil is definitely real, so we must be ready at all times to stand our ground against him. When I immediately spoke back to the devil and commanded him to flee, I regained strength and was able to persevere.

Some people might ask why they should have to go through so many terrible hardships. "Why me?" they question. My attitude is: "Why not me?" God will give us strength and cause us to mount up on wings like an eagle, so that we can soar again. When God is with you, you can go through fire and not be burned. There will not even be the smell of smoke on you.

It is God who sustains us. He loves us so much that He has engraved our names in the palm of His hand. He said, "My grace is sufficient for you. When I made you, I knew you would endure and that you would press on and not give up. I knew you before you were created in your mother's womb." He always knows best.

I thank God for men like Bishop T.D. Jakes who have been so instrumental in encouraging us women to be loosed and set free from the bondages and the chains of generational curses and soul ties that have held us back from going forth and encouraged us to lunch out in what God wants us to be.

Why Not You?

One day when I was in middle school, I said to my teacher, "I can't do that!"

She instantly replied to me, "I don't want to hear you use that word *can't* again. All can't comes in cans."

I never forgot those words. They have remained in my spirit throughout my lifetime. Now I know that nothing is impossible with God. He said that He has hidden secrets waiting for me that have not yet been revealed. So, I am searching for the deeper things of God.

I want more of God, more of His power, more of His strength, more of His wisdom and knowledge. Over the years, I have sought Him until now I realize I can be anything God wants to make of me. What I am now is not what I will be. He is still developing me.

I am on the Potter's wheel, and the work has just begun. There is more in me to be brought out, and there is more to be added to me to produce the wholeness He desires:

For which cause we faint not; but though our outward man perish, yet the inward man is renewed day by day. 2 Corinthians 4:16

Why Not a Woman?

When your inwards parts are being healed, your outward parts will show forth the workmanship that has been put into making you who God wants you to be.

There is Someone living on the inside of me Who is far higher and far greater than I could ever hope to be, and His presence in me is for a purpose. He is my Helper, and He has promised to send us the Comforter:

> *If ye love me, keep my commandments. And I will pray the Father, and he shall give you another Comforter, that he may abide with you for ever; even the Spirit of truth; whom the world cannot receive, because it seeth him not, neither knoweth him: but ye know him; for he dwelleth with you, and shall be in you. I will not leave you comfortless: I will come to you. Yet a little while, and the world seeth me no more; but ye see me: because I live, ye shall live also. At that day ye shall know that I am in my Father, and ye in me, and I in you. He that hath my commandments, and keepeth them, he it is that loveth me: and he that loveth me shall be loved of my Father,*

Why Not You?

*and I will love him, and will manifest myself
to him.*   John 14:15-21

The Helper will never leave us. He will live
in us every single day.

I accepted Jesus as a child, asking Him
to come into my heart at the age of nine. At
the time I didn't really understand all about
salvation, but what I did know was that I
wanted this Jesus I had heard others talking
about. I knew that I didn't want to go to Hell
Now, thank God, I know that He has prepared
for me a great destiny.

WHY NOT A WOMAN?
AND WHY NOT YOU?

Why Not A Woman?

She was fearfully and wonderfully made.
Why not a woman?
She was chosen to bring forth the Son of God.
Why not a woman?
She was chosen to lead an army when
her general refused to go without her.
Why not a woman?
She was chosen to be a man's helpmeet.
Why not a woman?
A weaker vessel, yet strong,
A wife, one who can be married
and belong to a man,
A mother, one who can give birth, to create,
to produce, to watch over,
nourish and protect,
A prophetess, a woman who speaks by divine
inspiration or as the interpreter through
whom the will of a God is expressed,
A missionary, one who is sent on a mission
WHY NOT A WOMAN?

She is generous, liberal in giving and sharing.
She is loyal, faithful to a person.
She is loving.
She doesn't just talk,
but embraces the situation.
She is a worker; her chores are never finished,
A laborer before God, prayerful.
WHY NOT A WOMAN?

Chapter 3

Know Who You Are

Henceforth I call you not servants; for the servant knoweth not what his lord doeth: but I have called you friends; for all things that I have heard of my Father I have made known unto you. John 15:15

One day I was in the break room at work, and a woman said to me, "Who do you think you are?" She touched a nerve and that gave me the opportunity to tell her about Jesus. I was in the Spirit that day and was not paying anyone much attention, but when she asked that question, I really lost it. I stuck my finger under my collar and turned to her and said, "I know who I am. I am fearfully and wonderfully made."

Then I heard someone saying, "Sit down, Vivian, sit down!" It was enough. I had allowed the love of God to flow and the Good News to come forth.

Know Who You Are

The Bible tells us that Abraham believed God, that it was imputed unto him for righteousness and that he was called the friend of God. I believe that God has also called me Friend. In fact, He has assured me that He will stick to me closer than any brother. I believe that God is just that close to me, and His love for me is just that deep. I have Someone who really loves me and really cares about me, and I am created in His image.

There is more. I am a part of the elect of God. Matthew 24:31 tells me: *"And he shall send his angels with a great sound of a trumpet, and they shall gather together his elect from the four winds, from one end of heaven to the other."* On that great day, my name, Vivian, will be called out, and yours will be too—if you are faithful to God. God will say, "Vivian, you have been faithful over a few things, I will make you ruler over many things; enter into the joy of the Lord."

Because of this, I am living in great expectation. Not only have I been chosen to be a worker in the Lord's vineyard and to show forth His praise, but I have a great future with Him. His Word declares:

Why Not a Woman?

For so hath the Lord commanded us, saying, I have set thee to be a light of the Gentiles, that thou shouldest be for salvation unto the ends of the earth. Acts 13:47

God has made me a light and has set me to lighten the way for others. As noted, He has told us:

Let your light so shine before men, that they may see your good works, and glorify your Father which is in heaven. Matthew 5:16

I am a proud beacon for my Lord. He has anointed me (see Luke 4:18) because there are many people who are broken, bruised and hurting who need to be delivered. Some have been taken captive in their minds, and they need to be set free. God has called you and me to go and preach the acceptable year of the Lord. Tell the people you meet of His love and why He died for them.

In that break room that day, a little light in me was burning and couldn't be quenched. It is a light that cannot be put out. Even when I am in the natural, I am a supernatural being. So I think supernatural thoughts because I serve a supernatural God.

There is another thing: I have been set aside and set apart for God's glory. This is not about you and me but about Him. He gets all the glory.

Are you one of His branches? Are you bearing fruit or just hanging on and about to fall off?

With all of this, I am a servant, not puffed up with pride and bragging, but with humility. Some of us, when we are asked to do something, can think of a dozen excuses why we cannot do it. God's Word, however says:

> *Whatsoever thy hand findeth to do, do it with thy might; for there is no work, nor device, nor knowledge, nor wisdom, in the grave, whither thou goest.* Ecclesiastes 9:10

Do it now, and do it to the glory of God!

We are not looking for our reward down here. We have a crown awaiting us, and whatever I have to do here to obtain that crown, I will do it. Of course I will!

Why Not a Woman?

I am a witness that Jesus died and rose again on the third day. I believe in the Trinity, the Father, Son and Holy Ghost. I am a witness that Christ died to save the lost. I am a witness that no sin can enter the Kingdom of God.

Romans 8:37 declares that I am more than a conqueror through Him who loved us. We have been give the power to pull down strongholds and tear the devil's kingdom down. We have been made kings and priest unto God. As ambassadors, we have been called out, set aside and set apart for the Kingdom for such a time as this.

I was made to bow down and worship the Creator. I was created to sing praise and glory to His name, that name which is above every other name. That's who I am!

Know that He is the Solid Rock that you can cling to when you go through troubled times. Know that He is the ever-living God, and He is not dead. Be assured that He is with you and you are safe in His arms. Be assured that He's your Shelter in the time of storm. Know that the God you trust in and believe in does glorious things. He is the sunshine after the rain, and He looks beyond all our faults and sees our needs. Know that one day Jesus paid it all when He hung on that cross and died for you and me. His blood was spilled for my sin and yours.

Tell me then,

WHY NOT A WOMAN?
AND WHY NOT YOU?

Chapter 4

Access to the Father

Therefore being justified by faith, we have peace with God through our Lord Jesus Christ: by whom also we have A C C E S S by faith into this grace wherein we stand, and rejoice in hope of the glory of God.   Romans 5:1

Access means "leading or bringing into the presence of; that which is associated with the thought of freedom to enter through the assistance of favor of another." Praise God, because I am highly favored! I am assisted by the favor of Christ to Father God. We cannot come to Him any other way but through His Son.

If it had not been for the cross and the shedding of Jesus' blood, I wouldn't have this freedom. Oh, but the veil has been rent, and I can now come boldly to the throne of grace and call on God freely. I can repent of my sins and know that there is forgiveness at the cross.

Access to the Father

In the past, I was in the flesh and couldn't make it, but once I was circumcised in the flesh, I was then ushered in. I now have access. Before, I was without Christ. I was an alien without Him. I was a stranger, and I didn't have any hope without God. I was afar off, but by His blood, I now have access. That wall that separated me from coming into His presence has been broken down, and now I have access. I am no longer a foreigner. Now I am a fellow citizen with the saints of God.

Now I can dance! I can shout! I can praise God! I can clap my hands and make a joyful noise unto the Lord without my heart condemning me because He tells me to come into His courts with praise and with thanksgiving on my mind.

This access which we have by faith through our Lord Jesus Christ is found in the early verses of Romans 5, where Paul went on:

Therefore being justified by faith, we have peace with God through our Lord Jesus Christ: by whom also we have ACCESS by faith into this grace wherein we stand, and rejoice in hope of the glory of God. And not only so, but we glory in tribulations also: knowing that tribulation worketh patience; and patience, experience; and experience, hope: and hope maketh not ashamed; because the love of God is shed abroad in our hearts by the Holy Ghost which is given unto us. Romans 5:1-5

My spirit man is at peace, and my mind is no longer troubled with the cares of this world. Why? Because Ephesians 3:12 declares:

In whom we have boldness and ACCESS with confidence by the faith of him.

There's that word *access* again.

Hebrews 10:19 agrees that I can enter with boldness into the Holiest by the blood of Jesus, for I have been loosed from my infirmities. Neither oppression nor depression can take me down the road of alcohol or drugs. And stealing, lying, cheating, fornication and adultery now have no hold over me. This is because I came to realize that I have access to the throne room, and I have been chosen, set aside, set apart for God's Kingdom.

I have been separated from the bondages of sin and death, and my grave clothes cannot hold me down any longer. I have that "Blessed Assurance" that Jesus is mine, that He is in me, and I am in Him.

What I am trying to say is this: You have to know who you are as a woman. And when you know, then why not a woman? Why not you? It's all in knowing who you are and what you have in Christ Jesus. I find that so many people don't know who they are and what they really possess. (For more study on this subject, I encourage you to read 1 John 2:28, 3:21 and 5:14-15.)

WHY NOT A WOMAN?
WHY NOT YOU?

Chapter 5

The Plan

This book of the law shall not depart out of thy mouth; but thou shalt meditate therein day and night, that thou mayest observe to do according to all that is written therein: for then thou shalt make thy way prosperous, and then thou shalt have good success.

Joshua 1:8

From the beginning of time, when God created man, He created him in His own likeness and image, and He saw that it was *"good."* God placed man and woman in the garden and blessed them and told them to multiply and replenish the earth and have dominion over it. Now, God could have chosen any other way, but He didn't. He chose you, and He chose you to bless you.

God told Adam and Eve, "I have given you every green herb bearing seed. And I will provide meat for you." Prepare for your harvest, for God will supply our every need. We shouldn't have a need if we are in Christ, and if we believe Him, trust Him and obey Him.

Man has always failed God, but God has always made provisions for man anyway. God makes ways for us when there seems to be no way. He creates pathways for us, and He leads us out to bring us into our expected end.

God told man in Joshua's day that he should observe to do according to all that was written, and if he did that, He would make his way prosperous, and he would have good success. That promise is still valid today. Still, God does not want you to be lazy or slothful; He calls you to be of good courage.

God promised that every place our foot would tread He would give it to us. Did you think that He only thought of the people of that day and left you and me out? No, there is a season of harvest for you and me as well.

Psalm 119 show us that God created man to praise Him, to bow before Him and to worship Him. In order for us to receive all the blessing

God has for us, we must learn how to touch the Father's heart.

David knew just what to do. He danced before the Lord. He bowed his knees before God. He shouted God's praises and didn't let anything or anyone stand in his way. Tell pride to step back, and tell you friends, "It's my time! I feel it, and I'm going for what's mine."

God will go every step of the way with you. He will never give up on you. He said that He would make the rough places plain and create a highway in the desert just for you.

There is an appointed time for you, and if I were you, I would do like that man who had been sitting around the pool for so long to get his healing. He sensed that his time had finally come, so he got in the water quickly (see John 5). There is a set time for your harvest. Why can't it be now? God is a now God.

God has told us not to worry. He told us not to let our hearts be troubled. He said He was going away, but that He would send us a Comforter.

He told us we can call upon Him at any time. He told us that blessings shall overtake us. We are under the same covenant that God promised to Abraham, Issac, Jeremiah and Joseph. God said:

> *In blessing I will bless thee, and in multiplying I will multiply thy seed as the stars of the heavens, and as the sand which is upon the sea shore: and thy seed shall possess the gates of his enemies.*   Genesis 22:17

God has always had a plan for man, from the beginning of time. That plan was for salvation, that man would not die, but live forever. And you are part of that plan.

Our God gave His Son that we may have abundant life. After man had fallen, Jesus became willing to give His own life to save a dying world and each and every lost man, woman boy and girl. So, the blessing is greater now than ever before, and all we have to do is go to the Father and ask. He is ready to bless you!

This salvation plan has always been from the beginning to the end, for God is Alpha and Omega.

- The plan was for you to prosper and be in health.
- The plan was for you to have plenty.
- The plan was for your soul to prosper.
- The plan was for you to increase in your finances.
- The plan was for you to lend and not borrow.
- The plan was to bless your family.
- The plan was that everyone who believes and receives should have eternal life.

And that's just the beginning. There is much more.

So, from the beginning to the end, the plan of salvation was that man (and, thank God, women) would live and not die, that man (and, thank God, woman) would live and reign with Him. That includes you!

**WHY NOT A WOMAN?
AND WHY NOT YOU?**

Chapter 6

Women in Action

Rise up, ye women that are at ease; hear my voice, ye careless daughters; give ear unto my speech. Isaiah 32:9

There were many great women in the Bible. Here are some examples.

MIRIAM

Miriam was a leader of God's people at a crucial moment in history. She led His people in celebration after they had successfully crossed the Red Sea, and she spoke God's Word to His people as she shared their forty-year journey through the wilderness on their way to the Promised Land.

DEBORAH

Deborah was one of the early judges. Her vision of the world was shaped, not by the politics of her day, but by her intimate relationship with God. Although women in the ancient world did not usually become political leaders, Deborah was just the leader Israel needed, a prophetess who heard from God and believed Him when He spoke. She brought her people great victory.

ESTHER

Queen Esther was an orphan in a foreign land, and yet she displayed great courage in a time of crisis. Prior to risking her life for her people, she humbled herself by fasting, and then she put her considerable beauty, social grace and wisdom to work in the service of God's plan. In the process, she saved her people and became Queen.

THE WOMAN AT THE WELL OF SAMARIA

When Jesus approached this woman, He broke through barriers of culture, race and religion to reveal Himself to her. When He had finished with her, she became an evangelist. "Come," she said "and see a man who told me everything."

Women in Action

PRISCILLA

Priscilla was one of the first Christians missionaries and a leader of the early Church, along with her husband Aquila. She risked her life for the apostle Paul. She was a woman whose spiritual maturity and understanding of the faith helped build the early Church. Her joy was to spread the Gospel and help mature the believers.

WHY NOT A WOMAN?
WHY NOT YOU?

- What has God spoken to your heart and spirit to do for Him?
- What are you waiting for to start spreading the Good News of Jesus Christ?
- Are you ready to be a witness for Him (see Ephesians 4:4-12)?
- In Matthew 28, Jesus commanded all of us, men and women alike, to go into all the world and spread the Good News of His salvation.
- In Mark 16:15, again, Jesus said, *"Go ye into all the world, and preach the gospel*

to every creature." He did not exclude women.

- Some may ask, "Shall I go, being a woman?" Yes! Why not? (see 1 Corinthians 12:12-31)

- God has said emphatically, in Romans 2:11, Ephesians 6:9 and 2 Chronicles 19:7, that there is no respect of persons with God. He can use whom He pleases. We must know when it is God, not just go on our own, and we must be led by the Spirit. But, by all means, go!

Women, we must know who we are in the Spirit. We know that God created man first and then created woman from man's side. Therefore we must also know how to be under authority. But, taking all of that into account, we must still ask ourselves:

WHY NOT A WOMAN?
AND WHY NOT YOU?

God's Favorite Woman

I am God's favorite Positive-
Confession Woman.
I am highly favored of the Lord.
There is favor all around me,
When I'm lying down and when I get up.
I think positively because my mind
is in tune with His mind.
My God is a positive God.
Therefore I am endued with favor
and positive emotions from above
Because His goodness and mercy
follow me wherever I go.

Chapter 7

Relation-Ships

And there arose a great storm of wind, and the waves beat into the ship, so that it was now full.   Mark 4:37

There are three important lessons you can learn about relationships by reading about three ships found in the Bible.

The first of those ships was Noah's Ark (see Genesis 6:9-8:22), and the lesson to be learned from it is this: Be careful who you get into a relationship with, for you may be sailing with that person for a very long time to come.

The eight people in the ark were together inside the limited confines of that ship for more than three hundred days, nearly a full year. Can you imagine the arguments they could have gotten into if they hadn't known how to get along with each other? The people you call friends should be willing to go the distance with you. Make sure you're willing to do the same for them.

The second lesson is found in the story of Jonah (see Jonah 1:1-4:11), and the lesson is this: Make sure the people you are in relationship with are going in the same direction God has told you to go.

Jonah got into a boat that was headed for Tarshish, and that was the opposite direction from where God had told him to go. Because he disobeyed God, a great storm arose and threatened the ship and everyone in it. In the end, Jonah had to be thrown overboard so that the other passengers and crew could be saved. Choose friends who are interested in God's plans. They will never throw you overboard. And be sure to do the same for them.

The third lesson concerns Jesus and His disciples crossing the Sea of Galilee (see Mark4:35-41), and the lesson is this: All relationships will go through storms!

Jesus went through a storm and His friends had to ride it out with Him. A true friend will stick with you when times get tough. If they can't calm the storm for you, at least they'll ride it out with you.

It is sad to say that you will lose some friends along life's way. This may cause you some hurt and pain, but always know that it is for your good. God always knows best.

WHY NOT A WOMAN?
AND WHY NOT YOU?

Chapter 8

Hurts

*Now when much time was spent, and when
sailing was now dangerous, because the fast
was now already past, Paul admonished them,
and said unto them, Sirs, I perceive that this
voyage will be with hurt and much damage,
not only of the lading and ship, but also of our
lives.* Acts 27:9-10

This know: disappoints will come, setbacks
will come, there will be misunderstandings,
and people you love will hurt you. This is just
part of life. Hurts happen.

Hurts are stressful and harmful. They result
from us feeling as though someone has treated
us wrong. Hurts come and hurts go in life, and
they often make you want to give up. Hurts
are also transferred. Because I am hurt, I then
want to hurt others. I want them to join with
my pain. I want them to feel what I'm feeling.

55

Why Not a Woman?

Surprisingly, suffering hurt brings about such things as lust, over-eating, illicit sex, shopping sprees, and many other negative things, and still the hurt is not satisfied.

Paul was on a ship sailing to Rome, but on the way, the ship, along with its passengers and crew, would encounter some hardships and some set-backs.

Hurts can result from the loss of some person or some thing. These can be so valuable to us or so close to us that the loss of them makes us want to bow to negative things. The devil knows this and tries to take advantage of it to get us to close up and just simmer in our hurt.

Hurts can bring about fear, and we often start to question ourselves, asking such things as "Why am I even here?," "Can I survive this loss?," maybe, "How did I get myself into this fix? and certainly "Why did this have to happen to me?"

Always remember that the devil is your adversary, and he would love to steal your mind, destroy what has been invested in you and even kill your spirit. Knowing that the joy of the Lord is your strength, Satan doesn't want you to have any joy, any strength or any peace. He would love to stop you in your tracks and make you feel that you can't possibly survive this loss.

Your enemy would love to kill your faith so that you would say, "I give up! Life is just not worth living!" Satan wants you to consider suicide or taking someone else's life. That's just what he does. Jesus said:

The thief cometh not, but for to steal, and to kill, and to destroy: I am come that they might have life, and that they might have it more abundantly. John 10:10

If Jesus is going to give me more abundant life, then the devil had better stand back. I will not allow the devil to steal what God has promised me.

In Acts 27:33-44, as Paul and the other passengers and crew were going through the storm, he addressed them all, urging them to eat something and assuring them that no harm would come to them. We must all pass through trials and tribulations, but they have a purpose. They are not to destroy us, but rather to strengthen us. If we can learn how to get into the flow of thanksgiving to God through faith, healing will flow to our troubled minds and broken hearts, and we will feel whole again.

Jesus wants us all healed, built up and strengthened in the power of His might. He came that we might be set free from every care.

Hurts can cause deep wounds, so deep that they cause bitterness that can last for a long time. It often seems as though we will never get over such a hurt. But God, who is rich in mercy, will deliver you and make you whole. Deliverance and healing is the children bread.

Sometimes, when other people lash out at you with their tongue, they may not even mean to hurt you. Realize that this is an attack of the enemy coming through them at you and resist it in Jesus' name. You will be victorious!

**WHY NOT A WOMAN?
AND WHY NOT YOU?**

Chapter 9

Walking in the Spirit of Forgiveness

There is therefore now no condemnation to them which are in Christ Jesus, who walk not after the flesh, but after the Spirit. For the law of the Spirit of life in Christ Jesus hath made me free from the law of sin and death.

Romans 8:1-2

This whole chapter of Romans talks about the life in the Spirit. I don't know about you, but I am one of God's lights, and I desire to walk in the light, for He is light. Now that this light is in me, I no longer desire to fulfill the lusts of the flesh, and we know what they are.

But along the way, someone or something is going to hurt you and cause you to need to ask for forgiveness. In your flesh lies *"no good thing"* (Romans 7:18), and you will be tested. If you walk in the Spirit, you will not fall. Why?

Why Not a Woman?

Because you have on the whole armor of God, and you depend on the Spirit to help you. In your time of need, always call on the Helper.

So, what does this have to do forgiveness and why must we walk in forgiveness? First, we must do it because Christ has forgiven us. In His model prayer recorded in Matthew 6:12-15, Jesus said that if we fail to forgive those who offend us, then our heavenly Father will not forgive us.

Then Jesus told how many times we needed to forgive (see Matthew 18:21-35), and it was more than once a day. Are you ready to walk in this truth?

Even if someone despitefully uses you, and you feel that you did nothing wrong, you need to forgive them anyway.

For if ye forgive men their trespasses, your heavenly Father will also forgive you.
                                        Matthew 6:14

Paul, writing to the Ephesians, said:

And be ye kind one to another, tenderhearted, forgiving one another, even as God for Christ's sake hath forgiven you.   Ephesians 4:32

Walking in the Spirit of Forgiveness

God loves others just as much as He loves us, and He will not hold you guiltless if you offend even one of them. Forgiveness is not for them; it's for you.

- Forgiveness frees us in the Spirit so that we can walk in the Spirit, move in the Spirit, and also so that we can sing and pray in the Spirit.
- Forgiveness lifts our burdens and removes our bondages and helps us to love in spite of what others might do.
- Forgiveness brings us into oneness with Christ.
- Forgiveness frees our mind, soul and spirit.

Many times I have had to forgive when I was deeply crushed and broken in my spirit by something someone had done to me. I had to learn to walk in the Spirit of forgiveness. Now, most of what was done to me I don't even remember. Forgiveness has made me free.

Sometimes forgiveness is not easy, and that's Satan's plan. I've had to forgive my father, my sisters, my sisters in Christ, my pastor, my friends, my son, my husband and you name it more.

Walking in the Spirit of forgiveness is the key because Jesus taught us how to forgive when He went through all that He did for us on the cross. His words were, *"Father, forgive them for they know not what they do"* (Luke 23:34).

Yes, my flesh wants to hold on to the hurts and make excuses why I cannot let them go. But I have found that *"I can do all things through Christ who strengths me"* (see Philippians 4:13). You must pray to the Father, just as Jesus did.

Sometimes we have to go back and face some of the giants in our lives in order to forgive. But be quick to forgive. Don't let the sun go down on your wrath (see Ephesians 4:26).

You might say, "But *I* didn't do anything; *they* did it to *me*." Jesus said, *"He that is without sin among you, let him first cast a stone"* (John 8:7). Are you without sin? Then get the beam out of your own eye before you try to get the mote out of someone else's (see Matthew 7:3-5). Forgive and you will be free.

Walking in the Spirit of Forgiveness

We must also learn to forgive ourselves Never stand and look in the mirror and accuse yourself. Seeing our own sin is not always easy, but if you look sincerely and long enough you'll find it. There is a lot wrong in your life, so be more concerned for the welfare of your own soul, and don't spend so much time judging others.

Here's an important question: Does forgiveness help you or the other person? It helps both, but it is more for you than for anyone else. Forgiveness warms the heart and cools the sting of offense.

I know that we all have read many articles and heard many sermons on the importance of forgiveness, but it is still not easy to put into practice. For most of us, forgiveness doesn't come easily.

And then there are the new hurts. Every time someone hurts us, we are left with a feeling of hurt, anger and vengeance. What does God have to say about it?

Dearly beloved, avenge not yourselves, but rather give place unto wrath: for it is written,

Why Not a Woman?

Vengeance is mine; I will repay, saith the Lord.

Romans 12:19

Still, we find it very difficult to let go of the hurts some people have caused us. We must understand that it's not about that person. This is the work of an evil spirit coming through them just to cause you to be angry and upset your spirit.

Forgiveness doesn't necessarily mean forgetting; it is just letting go of the hurt. It is not something you bestow on others, but a gift you give yourself. The hurt and pain someone has caused may always be a part of your life, but forgiveness will help loosen its grip on you so that you can move on.

And, as for whom to forgive, start with a friend who hurt you badly and a stranger who stepped on your toe on a bus. Then, in between those two extremes, forgive anyone and everyone who has offended you in any way.

Again, forgiving yourself is important. Forgiving quickly is also important because the more time you take to think about it, the more likely you are to never be ready to forgive. Do it as soon as possible. This may not change the past, but it will definitely change the future.

Remember: Not forgiving is like drinking rat poison and then waiting for the rat to die. This is dangerous. God cannot and will not dwell in an unclean vessel.

I must tell you a story of how hurt I was when I was a teenager. My dad had an extramarital affair, and it hurt my mother deeply, as it did the rest of the immediate family and the other side of the family as well. What he did was painful, disgraceful and shameful, and I didn't want to forgive him.

Did I love my dad? Yes, I did. It was the enemy who didn't want me to forgive him. Did I love my mother more than God. He warns us about that:

> *He that loveth father or mother more than me is not worthy of me.* Matthew 10:37

No, Mother had to fight her own battles. But as I grew in the Word and participated in a powerful church that taught on forgiveness,

Why Not a Woman?

I realized that my unforgiveness was not good and, thank God, I was able to allow Him to work in my life, so that I could drop everything that I was holding on to. Let go and let God change some things in your life. Be free through forgiveness.

We must learn from the things we experience in life. Everything is for our learning. Every single day God is teaching us how to stand in difficult times. We will go through some hard trials. David spoke of going through *"the valley of the shadow of death"* (Psalm 23:4). God was with him, and comforted and helped him.

Do I need God's forgiveness today? Yes, I ask Him to forgive me for the known, as well as the unknown, sins I have committed. And then I thank Him for everything He does for me. And He hears me.

When we walk in forgiveness, we can expect God to do wonderful things for us. We can expect to see situations changed and turned around for our good. Prayers are definitely answered when we forgive!

WHY NOT A WOMAN?
AND WHY NOT YOU?

Chapter 10

Establishment

And I, behold, I establish my covenant with you, and with your seed after you.

Genesis 9:9

I feel as though God wants to establish some things deep inside of you today.

In Exodus, God spoke seven times, and seven signifies completion. When God does something, He will complete it. God is not a halfway God is a God of completion. Nothing is half done with Him. He is a Finisher of things. When He made you, He made you whole and complete in Him. Here are some of the things He did and continues to do in you:

- He fearfully and wonderfully made you.
- He fills you with good things.
- He speaks to you.
- He sends you.

- He walks with you and talks with you.
- He feeds you.
- He clothes you.
- He put His Spirit deep inside of you and lives in you.
- He covers you.
- He goes before you and protects you.
- He loves you more than anything or anyone else can.

And that is just the beginning. What I am trying to say is that God is in covenant with His people. What He said He will do He will perform.

His Word is His covenant for us. This is why we need to read the Word, study the Word, eat the Word, and mediate on it day and night. It is a lamp to our feet and a light to our path and will lead us into all truth.

Then we will know and understand God's covenant for our lives. Then we can believe God for what we need and believe Him for all of His promises.

In Genesis 22:17, God was talking to Abraham, and I am a part of the seed of Abraham. God said:

Establishment

That in blessing I will bless thee, and in multiplying I will multiply thy seed as the stars of the heaven, and as the sand which is upon the sea shore; and thy seed shall possess the gates of his enemies.

I am a part of that inheritance!

God has always wanted to bless His people from the beginning to the end, but we have not kept the faith. We have not trusted Him. And we have murmured and complained too much.

I tell you today that God is waiting for you. He is waiting for you to step out of you comfort zone and put your trust in Him. Then your faith will produce your harvest.

In Deuteronomy 28, God said that He would bless us when we come in and also when we go out. He said that He would:

- Bless us in the city,
- Bless us in the country,
- Bless our fruits,
- Bless our seed,
- Bless our land,

- Bless our storehouses
- Bless and prosper everything we touch.

God wants to establish something in your heart today, for this is your season.

I am writing this to confirm some things in your life. God said that in no wise would you or I be put to shame. He promised that what He started He would finish. Rejoice, for this is your hour!

Ecclesiastes 3:1 says:

To every thing there is a season, and a time to every purpose under the heaven.

Verse 13 declares:

And also that every man should eat and drink, and enjoy the good of all his labour, it is the gift of God.

This is your season!

**WHY NOT A WOMAN?
AND WHY NOT YOU?**

Chapter 11

What Authority Do You Have?

And when he was come into the temple, the chief priests and the elders of the people came unto him as he was teaching, and said, By what authority doest thou these things? and who gave thee this authority?

Matthew 21:23

Do you realize how much authority you have? Do you really realize what God has given you? Do you really realize how much He has invested in you? Do you really realize who you are in Him?

Your faith should bring you into a deeper realm of the Spirit, to trust in Him and to believe that He is going to finish what He has started. What God has invested inside of you is good. He does not create bad things, only Satan does. God gives good gifts to His children, not evil.

Why Not a Woman?

First and foremost, God wants to anoint us. We have an absolute necessity of the Person and the work of the Holy Spirit within our lives. Jesus is the ultimate Anointed One, and the anointing of the Holy Spirit belongs to Him. The anointing we have actually comes by His authority.

Second, you need to know that you are sent, Who is sending you and what He is sending you for. He always sends us to lost sheep. Jesus said:

But go rather to the lost sheep.
Matthew 10:6

God knows what you will encounter before you set out on this journey. Some people, when they hit a snag, say, "That's a sure sign that God didn't send you." But that's not what God said. He said we would go forth *"as sheep in the midst of wolves"* (Matthew 10:16).

Are there wolves in the church? Oh, yes. Jesus continued to say to His disciples:

But beware of men: for they will deliver you up to the councils, and they will scourge you in their synagogues. Matthew 10:17

What Authority Do You Have?

You, like Paul, may have to go to jail for the sake of Christ. In the last part of verse 16, Jesus said:

Be ye therefore wise as serpents, and harmless as doves.

Thirdly, you need to know that God has given you power:

- Matthew 16:19 shows me that I have authority as a believer to use the name of Jesus. I can bind and loose, using the authority of that matchless name.
- Mark 16:17-18 shows me that I will do signs and wonders in that powerful name.
- Luke 10:19 shows me that I even have power over serpents and scorpions and that *"nothing"* can hurt me in Jesus' name. We can take dominion over every demon spirit and command it to go in Jesus' name.
- Matthew 4:1 shows me that even Jesus was tempted by the devil. It happened

three times, and each time He used His God-given authority to overcome.

Knowing that Jesus was hungry, the devil taunted Him that if He was the Son of God, He should turn stones into bread (see Matthew 4:3). And the enemy has not changed. He will test you to see if you know who you really are in Christ Jesus. This trick didn't work on Jesus. He knew His authority and used it to overcome, and you can too.

Next the enemy took Jesus up into the Holy City and set Him on the Pinnacle of the Temple, and said to Him, *"If you are the Son of God, cast yourself down"* (see Matthew 4:6). This is why we have suicides. When it happens, the devil is in authority. Well, that didn't work on Jesus either, and don't let it work on you.

Now desperate, the devil took Jesus and showed Him all the kingdoms of the world and said to Him, *"All this is Yours if you fall down and worship me"* (see Matthew 4:8-9). Jesus exercised His authority and said, *"Get thee behind me Satan, for it is written, You shall worship the Lord your God, and him only shall you serve"* (see Matthew 4:10).

What Authority Do You Have?

We must let the devil know, in no uncertain terms, that we believe God, we do not believe him, and we will never give in to his ways. Our authority is from above, and so we will have no other gods before us.

Jesus later said that the works He did we would also do and even greater works:

Verily, verily, I say unto you, He that believeth on me, the works that I do shall he do also; and greater works than these shall he do; because I go unto my Father. John 14:12

We live and move and have our being in this authority (see Acts 17:28), and therefore, we can command a thing in that authority, and it shall be done of our heavenly Father. We can walk in that kind of authority because God has promised to give us all the ground our feet tread upon.

WHY NOT A WOMAN?
AND WHY NOT YOU?

Be a Spirit-Led Woman

A Spirit-led woman is dangerous.
She is a threat to Satan
Because if you push her one way,
she'll come back another way.
She is strong and determined,
refuses to quit and is stable.
Stormy Omartian describes
her as a praying woman.
She gets God's attention.
The Proverb 31 woman is a praying woman.
She is going to attack the devil's territory,
Not only for family, but for the good of others.
Her aim is to win
because she knows who she is.

Chapter 12

Satan Will Try to Stop You

Wherefore we would have come unto you, even I Paul, once and again; but Satan hindered us.   1 Thessalonians 2:18

Did you know that the devil has plans for your life today? Any way he can possibly stop you from serving God, he will do it. It's his desire to steal from you, to steal your friends, your money, your family, and your joy and happiness. This is why we have so many people going around complaining, "I am a failure!" Satan has robbed them of life itself.

Your adversary wants to freeze you up to the point that you are overcome with fear. Then he can work on your nerves and you may start popping pills. At this point, you will be reaching for all sorts of medication.

He wants to kill your faith so that you will no longer believe in God's Word. "This

Word is not working for me," some say. He doesn't want you to gain knowledge and get understanding of the Word and why it might seem not be working in your life. Instead, he causes deafness and blindness to the truth. This is why sometimes we can't seem to pray or can't seem to be able to read the Word. Satan knows that God's Word will illuminate you, enlighten you and make you fruitful, so he will do everything he can to keep you from it.

Satan is determined to weaken you and make you feel that you have no strength to go on and receive what God has for you. God has good things in store for all of His children, and He has said that He withhold no good thing from you.

Other people, being used by Satan, will try to hinder you and keep you from going forth in what God has for you. This is where your faith must be active. You are trusting in the Lord, not in people. It is sad to see how Satan works through people, causing jealousy, envy, strife, gossip and malice.

Jesus said:

Satan Will Try to Stop You

Woe unto you, lawyers! for ye have taken away the key of knowledge: ye entered not in yourselves, and them that were entering in ye hindered. Luke 11:52

The people He was speaking to were supposedly experts in religion, but they actually hid the truth from people. They wouldn't accept it for themselves, and they prevented others from having a chance to believe.

Paul wrote to the Roman believers:

But as it is written, To whom he was not spoken of, they shall see: and they that have not heard shall understand. For which cause I have been hindered from coming to you. Romans 15:21-22

Even the great apostle Paul was hindered by Satan, but God will always make a way of escape. He will open doors where there seem to be no doors and make a way where there seems to be no way. The wise King Solomon wrote:

Why Not a Woman?

Trust in the Lord with all thine heart; and lean not unto thine own understanding. In all thy ways acknowledge him, and he shall direct thy paths.   Proverbs 3:5-6

God, who is rich in mercy, has our DNA and gives us His seal of approval. We are bought with a price, and so we are predestined to the Day of Redemption. Don't let anyone or any thing keep you from it.

WHY NOT A WOMAN?
AND WHY NOT YOU?

A Strong Black Woman

I'm a strong black woman.
Yes, that's me.
I'm strong and black phenomenally.
Can't no one stop my stride.
I'm a strong black woman,
And that I shall not hide.

I'm a hard-working woman, as you see.
I'm a hard-working woman phenomenally.
And anything you ask of me I will gladly do.
Willing to do whatever I can
to see you through.

I'm a one-in-a-million kind of woman,
and everyone knows
I carry Love, Strength and Peace
and it very well shows.
In spite of being knocked
down and talked about
by my so-called friends,
I've decided to keep on until the very end.

So, when you see me,
you will always see a smile.
And getting to know me will be
very well worth your while.
I'll continue to carry a smile
and never frown.

So, as I continue to do my thing,
And as I continue to be me,
know that I am a strong black woman,
and that I'm strong and black phenomenally.

Chapter 13

God Will Send an Angel

The angel of the LORD encampeth round about them that fear him, and delivereth them.

Psalm 34:7

In Daniel 6, a plot was hatched against the life of the Old Testament man of God known as Daniel. We know his story well. He was thrown into a den of lions because he was not willing to worship false idols, as the king had commanded. Who will you obey?

We know that the people who plotted against Daniel were of high office. They were jealous because Daniel was preferred above them. When you are walking with Jesus, you hold a high rank. Guard yourself well.

It is said of Daniel that he had an excellent spirit. Check your spirit. What kind of spirit do you have? Is it a spirit of meekness, love, joy, humility, graciousness or goodness? That's the type of spirit that pleases God.

Song of Solomon 8:6 warns, *"Jealousy is cruel as the grave."* These men really wanted to kill Daniel, and they thought they could achieve it by putting him into that lion's den. Surely he would be ripped apart. They couldn't wait. They intended to stand by laughing while it happened.

Isn't that just like the devil. That's exactly what he wants to do to us. But God sent an angel to help Daniel, and He will send an angel to help you too.

We know the enemy's plans. They are to kill, steal and destroy. But you have to know Who will deliver you. Know that God has angels encamped all about you:

God has also promised:

No weapon that is formed against thee shall prosper; and every tongue that shall rise against thee in judgment thou shalt condemn. This is the heritage of the servants of the LORD, and their righteousness is of me, saith the LORD.   Isaiah 54:17

God Will Send an Angel

Daniel was confident that the God He served was with him. How sure are you? Will you stand and be strong in the power of His might?

Jacob had an encounter with angels:

And Jacob went on his way, and the angels of God met him. And when Jacob saw them, he said, This is God's host: and he called the name of that place Mahanaim. Genesis 32:1-2

God will let you see how His Spirit is protecting you, if you are walking close to Him. The Lord pulled back the covers of the Spirit world and allowed Jacob to see the angelic host that accompanied him, and surely He will do the same for us.

In all their affliction he was afflicted, and the angel of his presence saved them: in his love and in his pity he redeemed them; and he bare them, and carried them all the days of old. Isaiah 63:9

This *"angel of his presence"* was the second Person of the Trinity and the highest Person of the angelic company, Jesus Himself. Didn't He say, *"I will never leave thee, nor forsake thee"* (Hebrews 13:5)? Didn't He say, *"Lo, I am with you always, even unto the end of the world"* (Matthew 28:20)? Didn't He say through the prophet Isaiah, *"Thou wilt keep him in perfect peace, whose mind is stayed on thee: because he trusteth in thee"* (Isaiah 26:3). Didn't He say through the prophet Jeremiah, *"Yea, I have loved thee with an everlasting love: therefore with lovingkindness have I drawn thee"* (Jeremiah 31:3). Is He not seated even now at the right hand of God making intercession for you?

> *It is Christ that died, yea rather, that is risen again, who is even at the right hand of God, who also maketh intercession for us.*
> Romans 8:34

So what seem to be our problem? God is letting us know, "I am with you." So, are you going to trust Him or trust someone or something else? Daniel trusted in his God. Was Jesus speaking to you when He said, *"O ye of little faith"* (Matthew 6:30)?

God Will Send an Angel

The prophet Elisha had an encounter with angels. He tried to encourage his servant:

And he answered, Fear not: for they that be with us are more than they that be with them.
2 Kings 6:16

What ditch have you fallen into? What trouble have you gotten yourself into? Even the great apostle Paul said that every time he tried to do good evil was present with him (see Romans 7:1). You have to know that there are some angels that have been dispatched to take care of you.

Your angel may only come at a certain season, but it will be right on time. You may be going through something, but there are more *for* you than there are *against* you.

An angel opposed Balaam (see Numbers 22:21-27) when he was doing something he should not have been doing. I believe that as we are walking along sometimes and we stumble, God is trying to tell us something. When I brush up against a wall or stub my toe, I sometimes ask myself, "Why is this happening?" God may be saying, "You didn't consult Me enough on this thing." His angels are there to protect us.

Unfortunately we are too often like Balaam, determined to do our own thing. "It has to be my way or no way." This is why we go through many heartaches. We are too hardheaded, like Balaam.

That angel stood in the road and tried to stop Balaam, but Balaam was determined to go where he had planned to go. His donkey had more sense than he did. Let's be more aware about what is really happening when things seem to be going wrong. Trust God to guide you into His very best for your life.

WHY NOT A WOMAN?
AND WHY NOT YOU?

Chapter 14

I Press

I press toward the mark for the prize of the high calling of God in Christ Jesus.

Philippians 3:14

The *mark* represents a moral and spiritual target. The *high calling* is a Christlikeness, which proclaims the manner and means by which all of this is done, which is through the cross of Christ.

You and I must come to a place in life where we take a stand and say, "I press with determination. I will press through every situation, no matter what I happen to be going through at the moment." Tests and trials will erupt, causing all sorts of chaos in our lives, but this is where we must stand:

1. Verse 8 of that chapter speaks of pressing for *"the excellently of the knowledge of*

Christ." As I am pressing forward for more, I can have companionship with Him.

2. Verse 9 speaks of pressing *"that I may be found in him."* In Christ, I have His joy, His peace, His love, His happiness, His wisdom and His knowledge. This is all true because the light of Christ is in me. Without Him, I would be in utter darkness.

3. Verse 10 speaks of pressing *"that I may know Him."* I want His mind in me. Then there will be a humility and a willingness about me that I am not capable of on my own.

What are some of the characteristics that help us to press for more in God?

- Isaiah 57:15—When you are a humble person, you free God to manifest Himself to you and through you.
- Judges 7—When you are obedient, you free God to do mighty acts through you.
- Colossians 3:22-24—God will make you free so that He can reward you divinely.

- Genesis 39-41—When you are loyal, you free God to promote you. You are no longer on milk but on strong meat.

- Matthew 25:21—When you are faithful, you free God to expand your mind, your thoughts and all other aspects of your life. God has said that if we are faithful over a few things, He will make us ruler over many.

- Habakkuk 2:1—When you are watchful, you free God to speak to you. We all want to hear Him when He calls us. It may be to pray or it may be to go.

- Daniel 6:23—When you are courageous, you free God to help you and protect you. Be bold and be strong in the power of His might. Believe God for guidance in every little thing.

- Luke 10:41-42—When you are not quarrelsome, angry, bitter or jealous (these things must be put away), then you are free to focus and you free God to focus on what He wants to do in your life.

- Luke 22:32—When you are gentle, you free God to strengthen you and remove everything out of the way that may cause a hindrance. Call out to Him: "Lord, I need You to strengthen me in this battle, for I cannot do it without You. I need You Lord, right now." No battle is too hard for God.

- Matthew 7:28-29—When you are able to teach, you free God to establish divine order in your life. *"Study to show thy self approved unto God, a workman that needeth not to be ashamed, rightly dividing the word of truth"* (2 Timothy 2:15). Pray, "Lord, Your will and not mine. I have been doing it my way too long."

- John 14:8-14—When you are patient, you free God to answer your prayers. And we all want our prayers answered.

Pause right now and ask God, "Is there something in me that is hindering Your work?" Then ask Him to remove anything and everything that is blocking your prayers from reaching His throne room. Pray:

Lord, here I am, coming before You, asking You, Lord, to search my heart, my mind, my thoughts and to give me a clean heart.

Lord, I come to You because I know You already know everything about me because You made me. Here I am, O God, coming humbly before You. You told me to cry out and spare not (see Isaiah 58:1), so I lay myself at the foot of the cross. Here am I. I come because You said, *"Come unto me all ye that labour and are heavy laden, and I will give you rest"* (Matthew 11:28).

Father, I come to rest in You, recognizing that I am Your child, and I need You to do Your perfect will in me. I'll wait on You, pressing so that I may attain. This means the newness of life in Christ Jesus.

Amen!

We all want the freshness of God every day, and we want to be thankful for what He is doing every day. Even though we may not see it, He is at work in us. So we press.

- Psalm 2:5-9—When you are meek, you free God to guide you. I press because I have not reached perfection as yet, but I am yet striving.

• Matthew 7:17—When you are good, you free God to produce fruit in you. We all want to be productive, to bring forth the things that are pleasing in God's sight. The first of those, of course, is LOVE. People are so much in need of love these days and it stinks because we don't know how to love. We have been hurt so much and have not been healed from the wounds and the scars. The goodness God places in us is productive. God has put some good qualities in us so that we can be a blessing to others. I press so that I can stay focused on the things of God. I press to keep the faith and not give up, because I realize that I am in a battle, there is a war going on inside of my members. I must fight the good fight of faith; so, I press.

• Matthew 24:25—When you are wise, you free God to invest in you with authority. He has given us the authority to decree a thing and it shall be done. He has given us the authority to command our day. He has given us the authority to go and do His bidding. This is all part of being a wise woman. Think of the ten virgins. Five of them were foolish, and five were wise. Five made sure they had enough oil in there lamps, and five didn't. Think about the Proverb 31 woman. She knew what she had to do to keep her home intact. Have you read about the wise woman of Abel? She was able to successfully intercede for her town, thus averting disaster for many innocent people. Rather than passively waiting for someone else to save her city, she had the wisdom and courage to act quickly and decisively. You and I need to ask God for wisdom every single day.

All these characteristics will help us to get to what we are pressing toward, and that is to ultimately reach that heavenly home that is prepared for each of us.

WHY NOT A WOMAN?
AND WHY NOT YOU?

A Strong Woman

*A strong woman won't let
anyone get the best of her!*

*A woman of strength gives the
best of herself to everyone!*

*No matter how many rocks she has stumbled
on, her faith and strength remain intact!*

Chapter 15

I Won't Leave You

And, behold, the LORD stood above it, and said, I am the LORD God of Abraham thy father, and the God of Isaac: the land whereon thou liest, to thee will I give it, and to thy seed; and thy seed shall be as the dust of the earth, and thou shalt spread abroad to the west, and to the east, and to the north, and to the south: and in thee and in thy seed shall all the families of the earth be blessed. And, behold, I am with thee, and will keep thee in all places whither thou goest, and will bring thee again into this land; for I will not leave thee, until I have done that which I have spoken to thee of.

Genesis 28:13-15

There is a saying that faith neither steps forward nor backward, but holds the hand which says: "Certainty I will be with you." So if you have the faith that Jesus will always be with you, you won't ever want to be without Him. God has always promised His children that He will be right there.

In Genesis 28:13-15, we have read what God said to Jacob:

1. God said, "I am with you." Jesus added to this, *"I tell you the truth; It is expedient for you that I go away: for if I go not away, the Comforter will not come unto you; but if I depart, I will send him unto you"* (John 16:7).
2. God said, "I will keep you."
3. God said, "I will bring you." He will bring us to our expected end, if we keep the faith and expect Him to do the rest.
4. God said, "I won't leave you." You may be experiencing some hard times, but go on through, for God is right by your side. All God was and still is asking of us is to be obedient. He will do the rest!

When you are going through your trial, your pain or whatever situation it may be (which we are all known to have), God has said in Psalm 32:8: *"I will guide thee with mine eye."* He will guide us until the end. By allowing us to pass through some afflictions, He is just trying to strengthen us, to make us stronger. Then, when the enemy comes in like a flood, you will be able to stand.

I know what I'm talking about, for I have been through some serious tests and trials. I have heard the devil telling me to give up. It is his business to approach us at our lowest point.

I lost my mother in 1971. As a young girl, I had done all that I could for her, so the devil was not able to make me bow over her passing.

Daddy never got over Mom's death, so he proceeded to drink himself to death over the next seven years.

I thought I could deal with Daddy's death, but then my husband died a month before Dad's death. When my husband passed, Dad had promised that he would be there for me, to assist me in any way I needed him. Now he, too, was gone, and all I had was God.

In the space of six months, I lost five family members, and just the thought of death turned me cold. I didn't want to hear about any more funerals.

Why Not a Woman?

"What's next?" I wondered. What was next was that my baby boy went to jail for life on a murder charge, and that was when I met Satan face to face. He said to me, "Are you ready to serve me now because I have taken something so dear to your heart?"

I looked up and said, "Lord, I will serve You."

Did I fall during this ordeal? Yes, the devil knew I loved that child so much, but what he had done totally crushed me. However, I never gave up on God. I held on to the altar and called on Him many times.

I was hurting so badly, and the devil would come to throw all of his fiery darts, to try and make me give up. I knew in my heart that I loved God more than anything else and that He was living in me. God knows our hearts. I had always maintained the determination to serve the Lord all of my days.

Until this day, I don't want to be without Him. He has been my strength. I don't know exactly what lies ahead, but this one thing I know: God is going to see me through as He has so faithfully done in the past.

I Won't Leave You

During that ordeal, I was offered cocaine. I heard the Spirit say NO, and I walked away. The devil will tempt you with whatever he thinks can cause you to stoop. The Bible warns us to be aware of Satan's devices (see 2 Corinthians 2:11). I realized that the devil wanted me to bow to him, but I would not. I am a happy and joyous person, and my victory was all won at the cross through the blood of Jesus Christ.

Sometimes I hear a song in my spirit:

I trust in God, I know He cares for me;
On mountain bleak or on the stormy sea;
Though billows roll, He keeps my soul;
My heav'nly Father watches over me. [1]

I pray that you feel Him as I do as I am writing this. When you start to praise God, it touches His heart, and He lends His ear to hear. He created us to worship Him.

Sometimes I love to sit down with hurting people, especially women, and hear their hurts and their pain and let them know that there is hope. We encourage each other in the Lord.

---

1. Written by Charles H. Gabriel in 1910. Public Domain.

Why Not a Woman?

This is what Jesus told us to do: to love through, to show love. Let your love be active. Don't just say it. Be a doer.

One day I heard the voice of the Lord speak to me, and He brought me to Luke 4:18-19:

The Spirit of the Lord is upon me, because he hath anointed me to preach the gospel to the poor; he hath sent me to heal the brokenhearted, to preach deliverance to the captives, and recovering of sight to the blind, to set at liberty them that are bruised, to preach the acceptable year of the Lord.

The Lord went on, "Know who you are as a woman, that you are the weaker vessel. But, in Christ, you are strong. Learn how to rely on the Word of God to give the strength you need to go through what you are facing in life."

Many times, when I am reading or studying my Bible and I hear the Spirit speaking to me, I realize that it is a personal thing, so I jot my name there beside it. All through my Bible you will find my name on various scriptures. I have claimed them as my own.

I Won't Leave You

For instance, when I lost my husband, it was devastating. We had been so close and had walked together through so much. Now the Word came to me in Joshua1:2-18, the whole chapter. God said, "George [my husband] is dead. Vivian, you go on now. Every place that the sole of your foot shall tread upon, that have I given unto you. Vivian, I will not fail you, nor forsake you. Vivian, be strong and of good courage. Vivian, only be thou strong and very courageous. Vivian, have not I commanded you? Be strong and of good courage; be not afraid, neither be dismayed for the Lord thy God is with you whithersoever you go."

He repeated it again in the last verse: "Vivian, only be strong and of good courage." God knows us by name, He speaks to us individually, and He is our ever-present comfort.

Jesus made this clear when He was nearing the end of His time here on Earth. He said to His disciples:

Go ye therefore, and teach all nations, baptizing them in the name of the Father, and of the Son,

*and of the Holy Ghost: teaching them to observe
all things whatsoever I have commanded you:
and, lo, I am with you always, even unto the
end of the world. Amen.* Matthew 28:19-20

That final Amen! was the confirmation that
God would never leave us. And this promise is
for you today!

**WHY NOT A WOMAN?
AND WHY NOT YOU?**

Chapter 16

Never

Let your conversation be without covetousness; and be content with such things as ye have: for he hath said, I will NEVER leave thee, nor forsake thee. Hebrews 13:5

NEVER is a word that we often say very fast but don't give much thought to. It's such a small word that we don't put nearly enough emphasis on it. We might call it a "fly-by" word. We say it, but when we do, we don't stop to think what we're really saying.

We use the word *never* when we get married, but still we have way too many divorces. We often say that we will *never* do this or that, and then we do it. I wonder how God looks upon us when we use (or misuse) the word *never*.

God knows what we are going to say, but He also know what we are going to do. Are we going to do what we say?

Why Not a Woman?

Think about it! Before you ever used this powerful and often-misused word, God said it. *Never!* The difference is that when God says something He means it. When He says it, you can count on it. It will be done.

NEVER means not ever or not at any time!
NEVER is non-existent!
NEVER is eternal!

And NEVER is an oath made by God to His people. Have you made the same oath to Him?

Some may try to hold their breath with this word, but they cannot because never has no ending. Our God is the Alpha and the Omega, the Beginning and the End (see Revelation 1:8 and 11, 21:6 and 22:13). He is eternal. There is no end to Him. He always was and always will be—forever and ever.

That's why we have such a great hope. Our God will never die. He will never leave us. He will never fade away. He is alive, ever-living and ever-present.

God is saying to you today, "I will never leave you. I will never abandon you." Know this in your heart, for it is a certainty. It is His promise.

The Bible says that God has engraved our names upon the palms of His hands (see Isaiah 49:16). His eye is continually on us, and He is watching over us. His arms are ever present to comfort us in times of need.

When Peter saw Jesus walking on the water of the Sea of Galilee, he wanted to go meet His Lord, but he was afraid. Then Jesus said a simple word to Peter, *"Come"* (Matthew 14:29), and suddenly all fear was gone. Peter also began to walk on the sea.

At one point, however, Peter took his eyes off of Jesus and, seeing the winds and angry waves, he began to sink. But all he had to do was cry out to Jesus, and the Lord was there to save him. Fear cannot overcome us when we know that God will never leave us.

When Jesus went back to Heaven, He left us great promises. One of those promises was that He was going away to prepare a place for us. If we believe Him, knowing that He would never lie to us, we can have peace in this world. God is preparing a place for us in eternity.

Why Not a Woman?

God has promised never to forsake us, never to leave us helpless. He has promised to send the Comforter to help us with every step of the way. This promise from God was true in days of old:

And David said to Solomon his son, Be strong and of good courage, and do it: fear not, nor be dismayed: for the LORD God, even my God, will be with thee; he will not fail thee, nor forsake thee, until thou hast finished all the work for the service of the house of the LORD.
1 Chronicles 28:20

As noted, Jesus made it clear that this promise was still in effect today:

Lo, I am with you always, even unto the end of the world. Amen!   Matthew 28:20

That promise stirs my spirit and makes me want to cry out to God all the more, telling Him how very much I love Him. How awesome our God is to us!

Never

I must refer again to the day my husband George passed away. As you can imagine, that was a very traumatic day for me. If you have never experienced the sudden loss of a loved one, you cannot imagine how it feels. Suddenly the one I had loved and who had loved me was gone, and there was a great vacuum in his place.

As I noted earlier in the book, the very next day the Lord took me to the first chapter of Joshua and began showing me how to go on.

Moses my servant is dead; now therefore arise, go over this Jordan, thou, and all this people, unto the land which I do give to them, even to the children of Israel. Joshua 1:2

As I read this, God said, "George, My servant is dead; now you go on, Vivian." Please read this whole chapter carefully. There is so much in there for every believer.

That sounded so good to me that I read on:

Every place that the sole of your foot shall tread upon, that have I given unto you, as I said unto Moses. Joshua 1:3

Why Not a Woman?

As I read that, God said, "Every place that the sole of your foot shall tread upon, Vivian, I have given it to you."

I came to verse 5:

There shall not any man be able to stand before thee all the days of thy life: as I was with Moses, so I will be with thee: I will not fail thee, nor forsake thee.   Joshua 1:5

As I read that, God said, "There shall not any man be able to stand before thee all the days of thy life, Vivian: as I was with Moses, so I will be with thee: I will not fail thee, nor forsake thee."

I read verses 6 and 7:

Be strong and of a good courage: ... Only be thou strong and very courageous, that thou mayest observe to do according to all the law, which Moses my servant commanded thee: turn not from it to the right hand or to the left, that thou mayest prosper whithersoever thou goest.   Joshua 1:6-7

Never

As I read that, God said, "Be strong and of a good courage, Vivian. Be strong and very courageous, Vivian, that thou mayest prosper whithersoever thou goest." Oh, I'm so glad He knows my name and that He calls me by name! Because His promises are for me, I have taken the liberty of writing in my name throughout the Bible. Those promises are mine, so why should I not claim them?

The chapter ended with more assurances and an encouraging word:

Only be strong and of a good courage.
Joshua 1:18

As I read that, the Lord said, "Vivian, only be strong and of a good courage." I knew then that any battle I might have to fight, anything that I might have to go through, He would be right there helping me and encouraging me on. I could make it. It had seemed that I was suddenly alone, but I was not alone. The Creator of the Universe was with me.

All I needed to do was keep looking unto Jesus, the Author and Finisher of our faith. The race would not be to the swift, the battle would not be the strong nor would bread and riches be to the wise and understanding (see Ecclesiastes 9:11). As Jesus said, those who endured to the end would be saved (see Matthew 10:22).

You must come to realize that God is always with us no matter what we may go through. He will never leave us. This means that the battle is not ours. It is the Lord's, and He will fight for us.

WHY NOT A WOMAN?
AND WHY NOT YOU?

Chapter 17

It's Not Too Late!

And God said unto Abraham, As for Sarai thy wife, thou shalt not call her name Sarai, but Sarah shall her name be. And I will bless her, and give thee a son also of her: yea, I will bless her, and she shall be a mother of nations; kings of people shall be of her. Genesis 17:15-16

It is a blessing when God joins together a man and a woman in holy matrimony, and as they join together they both strive to obey God in their daily lives. It is a blessing to see the progress they make. You can see God's blessing on them, and how wonderful that is!

When we look at the life of Abraham and Sarah of old, we see that God told Abraham five times in Genesis 17:1-8 that he would have a son. He spoke to Sarah five times in Genesis 17:15 and told her the same thing. She laughed and asked, "In my old age?" But there is a definite and special blessing when two people are walking in agreement one with another and also with their God.

Even though Abraham and Sarah were past the normal child-bearing age, God's promises were still upon them. It wasn't too late, even at ninety-nine.

Abraham was a man of faith, and he believed God. But we must realize that God's timing is not our timing. We want things instantly, and we're always in a great hurry. We don't like the idea of waiting for anything. When we have to wait for any reason, we easily tire and get frustrated and want to give up.

According to Judges 2:1, the Lord never breaks His covenant with us.

And an angel of the Lord came up from Gilgal to Bochim, and said, I made you to go up out of Egypt, and have brought you unto the land which I sware unto your fathers; and I said, I will never break my covenant with you.

Judges 2:1

Unfortunately, we do break our covenant with God. We sometimes make promises to

Him that we know we're not going to keep. God wants us to be honest with Him, and if we are, He will show us that it is never too late for His promises to be revealed.

Psalm 32:8 lets us know that, no matter what things seem like and no matter how bad our situation may seem, as long as we are not rebellious, He will instruct us, teach us, and guide us with His eye. God told David that He would deliver him in times of trouble, and God is saying to us that we can't be too old or too young for Him to carry out His promises for us.

No, it's not too late. There is a right timing in God. In the meantime, there are things that God is working out in you, and He is allowing things to happen to get your attention. Sometimes we get caught up in our own ways and move so fast that God can't lead us with His eye.

Perhaps you have always wanted to go out and do things for God but have been frustrated. I have no way of knowing what has held you back, but I do know that God has a plan for you. First, you must know who you are and what His desire for you is.

Why Not a Woman?

Have you ever sat down and asked God to show you who you really are? Many people haven't, and that is a big problem. When you know who you are, then you can get very personal with God, very intimate with Him, and the two of you can communicate better. Now, you're not just reading the Bible; you are having a personal talk with God.

It's not too late for any of us to take the Good News into the highways and byways. Be determined to be all that God wants you to be. Recognize that you are here for a purpose, and the main purpose of your existence is to glorify your heavenly Father.

God tells us to seek Him with all our heart, mind and soul (see Deuteronomy 4:29), and it is up to each of us to seek Him for what He has for us. We are each part of the Body of Christ, and every part has a purpose and should be in working order.

Yes, people will question you and call you crazy. Just tell them what God's Word says, that there is salvation only in the name of Jesus Christ and that He must always be first in our lives. It can be no other way, for without Him we can do nothing.

It's Not Too Late!

As noted earlier, God told us in Matthew 10:16, *"Behold I send you forth as sheep in the midst of wolves, be ye therefore wise as serpents and harmless as doves."* In the days of Peter and John, the people saw their boldness and were attracted to them because of it. And, because you are a child of the living God, there must also be a boldness in you.

I have been traveling to the mission fields of Africa and other places for the past thirteen years. I had always wanted to go, but I didn't know how or when. I had to call on God and believe Him to open the doors for me.

What I liked most about visiting these mission fields was getting to know the culture. I love the people, no matter what nationality they are of, and I want to give them my love. I want to eat what they eat and then share with them the Good News of Jesus.

I had long wanted to get out of my comfort zone and feel what it was like not to be in my own bed. Believe me, it was not easy, but many times this is when God really speaks to us, when we need to depend on Him more. We are a nation of spoiled people.

Why Not a Woman?

Your mission may not be Africa, but whatever the task God has for you, it's not too late. Rest in Him, and be assured that He is with you, He will never leave you, and He will take you all the way.

Paul declared to the Corinthian Church:

And such trust have we through Christ to God-ward: not that we are sufficient of ourselves; but our sufficiency is of God; who also hath made us able ministers of the new testament; not of the letter, but of the Spirit; for the letter killeth, but the Spirit giveth life.

2 Corinthians 3:4-6

Doubters need not apply. We need believers in Christ Jesus.

It's not too late to receive your healing. It's not too late to see souls saved in your lifetime. It's not too late for God to show Himself mighty on your behalf. Just be willing, ready and obedient.

God is calling us to be hunters and fisherman in this beautiful garden that He has placed us in to cultivate. He declares:

It's Not Too Late!

The harvest truly is great, but the labourers are few: pray ye therefore the Lord of the harvest, that he would send forth labourers into his harvest. Luke 10:2

Maybe you have been guilty of saying, "It's too late, it just not happening," but let God have the last say. His ways are not our ways, and IT'S NOT TOO LATE!

WHY NOT A WOMAN?
AND WHY NOT YOU?

Chapter 18

Increase

We beseech you, brethren, that ye INCREASE more and more.

1 Thessalonians 4:10

To increase means "to grow," and God wants us all to grow—naturally and spiritually. Did you think that God made you to be the same always? No! God wants us to be lively stones, to constantly grow and become greater. He wants us to be active. Salt that has lost its savor is good for nothing (see Matthew 5:13).

There should be no stagnation in you, because the Word of God should be like fire shut up in your bones. There must be growth taking place in you always. You are no longer on milk, but you are now able to digest strong meats and are being built up in your holy faith.

Your mind is now stronger, and you can think on those things that are pure, those things that are of a good report (see Philippians 4:8). Now, when the devil tries to come with his evil thoughts, you can be strong enough to brush them off. You are able to cast down wrong imaginations and pull down things in high places. You can rise up in your spirit man and say, "No weapon formed against me shall prosper, for greater is He that is in me than he that is in world." Now God will cause you to soar like an eagle.

We are also to increase in abundance, in our substance, in our finances. The admonition of 1 Thessalonians 4:10, that we *"increase more and more,"* is followed by another, in verse 12, *"that ye may have lack of nothing."* Since this is God's Word, we can conclude that God Himself does not want us lacking in anything. He promised:

But my God shall supply all your need according to his riches in glory by Christ Jesus.   Philippians 4:19

No good thing will he withhold from them that walk uprightly.   Psalm 84:11

121

God owns it all, and He wants us to enjoy it. He said that what we make happen for someone else (when we cry out to Him), He will pour the same blessing back on us.

In Malachi 3:10-11, He told us to bring all the tithes and offerings into the storehouse that there may be meat—plenty of it!

Then God tells us how to give. He said we should not give grudgingly or out of sorrow that we have given, but we should come before the Lord with a cheerful heart, knowing it is He who has blessed us and He who is our substance.

Every man according as he purposeth in his heart, so let him give; not grudgingly, or of necessity: for God loveth a cheerful giver.
2 Corinthians 9:7

Just as God has given you what you turned around and gave back to Him, He can bless you with much more than that. He blesses when He choses and whom He choses. And this is your season of harvest!

When Joseph's brothers put him in that waterless pit, they weren't quite sure what to do with him. What they knew was that they hated him and were jealous of him. When they saw a company of Ishmaelites passing by, this seemed like the perfect solution. They wouldn't have to kill him themselves. They could sell him to the Ishmaelites and let them do whatever they wanted with him. Wow! Look what your family will do to you! But if God be for you, who can be against you?

This treachery affected Joseph just like it would you. He missed his father. He was treated like a slave, so he missed the comforts of his own home. Then he was put in prison. Amazingly, through it all, Joseph prospered. God will increase you in due time, and you shall reap—if you faint not.

Because you are in Christ, the devil will have to bow, and God will exalt you in due time. Pharaoh recognized the truth about who Joseph was and set him over the land of Egypt. He took off his own ring and placed it on Joseph. He dressed Joseph in fine linen and placed a gold chain around his neck. Joseph was able to feed his entire family during the coming famine. God will fight for you in your time of struggle.

Why Not a Woman?

Later, when the Israelites had left Egypt and were building the wilderness Tabernacle, Moses received an offering from the people. They brought an offering every morning. Eventually, however, it was more than what was needed and Moses had to say, "These people have brought more than enough for the work of the sanctuary" (see Exodus 36). Amazingly, he had to send out word for the people to please stop giving. What a blessing!

Please don't ever get tired of giving to God, for God has given His all for you. All of your giving will pay off in time. You simply cannot outgive God, and He has destined you for increase!

WHY NOT A WOMAN?
AND WHY NOT YOU?

Chapter 19

My Season of Harvest

Lift up your eyes, and look on the fields; for they are white already to harvest. John 4:35

Why do I claim that this to be my season of Harvest? You must believe in you heart that God's love for you is everlasting, and there is no shortness in Him. You must believe that you are positioned for such a time as this. This a season of breakthrough, so why not your breakthrough?

Although the struggles may have been hard at times, still I press to receive all that God is and will be. Again, there is no shortness in Him. Therefore, I should not be experiencing shortness either.

God has instructed me to be holy as He is holy. He took His time when He was making me in His own image. He is the One who has kept the air flowing through my nostrils and the blood flowing through my veins, and truly I am fearfully and wonderfully made.

He said He would withhold no good thing from those who walk upright before Him. So, here I am, Father, like a little bird in its nest, waiting for Your outpouring.

God wants our humility. He said:

Humble yourselves therefore under the mighty hand of God, that he may exalt you in due time. 1 Peter 5:6

As we humble ourselves and wait in His presence, blessings will come:

- I am waiting for the overflow of His mercy and grace in my life.
- I am waiting for the windows of Heaven to open and overflow onto me.
- I am waiting for my healing.
- I am waiting for my household to be saved.
- I am waiting for His promise that I am a lender and not a borrow. I am waiting for His plenty.

My Season of Harvest

As I wait, I say:

I know that You are God, and You don't lie. Whatever You have said You will perform. I stand guard and in position, as the unveiling of my season of harvest is unfolding.

I realize that my season of harvest may come in many ways. It may come financially, spiritually and/or physically. You said that You would open up the windows of Heaven and pour out a blessing greater than I could contain. I trust You and await Your blessing.

As I wait before You, every demon force must stand back. You have given me power over Satan, and he is under my feet. I am able to move forward without interference, trampling under foot anything that tries to stand in my way.

I am divinely positioned. As we have noted, no weapon that is formed against me shall prosper, and everything that rises up against me shall fall (see Isaiah 54:17). I am the

righteousness of God (see 2 Corinthians 5:21),
I am His mouth-piece, going forth to take back
what the devil has stolen.

This is my season of harvest, my time to
reap, my time to be blessed. Why not yours
too?

As we have noted, God's Word declares:

*To every thing there is a season, and a time to
every purpose under the heaven.*

Ecclesiastes 3:1

This is my season, and I am waiting and
expecting, because my God owns the cattle on
a thousand hills (see Psalm 50:10). Will you do
the same?

**WHY NOT A WOMAN?
AND WHY NOT YOU?**

Chapter 20

You Can't Walk in My Shoes

And ye shall not walk in the manners of the nation, which I cast out before you: for they committed all these things, and therefore I abhorred them. Leviticus 20:23

How many pairs of shoes have you purchased in your lifetime? How did you walk in those shoes? Did you walk sideways in them? Did you walk backward or did you walk the right way in them all the time? We are imperfect beings, so we are not always the same. Ours is a faith walk.

What color shoes did you buy? Some of us don't like certain colors. Our tastes change over time, and God didn't give us all the same tastes to begin with. Some of us like dark colors, and others prefer lighter colors. But whatever the color or no matter how heavy the load you are called to carry, we must all face up to whatever shoes we are given in life to wear.

To you, the shoes you have been given may feel too big or too wide, but God knows best. Trust Him. The shoes you have been given may hurt your feet or pinch. But, whatever the problem you have with the shoes you have been given, wear them with dignity. They have been built just for you, and they will lend you strength in the long run.

Your shoe may be way too big for me, but God knows just what size I need. My shoes might be too wide for you and will not fit your feet. If so, they wouldn't stay on your feet or be comfortable for you to wear. Believe me, God does all things well. Some of us wear narrow, medium, large or extra large. Whatever size you wear, that's the size you must stick with. Wear it with dignity. God knows just how much we can each bear, and He won't put any more in these shoes than we can successfully carry.

Your shoes may carry you in sunshine for a long while, but there will come a time in your life when a little rain must fall. Then, when the flood comes, those shoes may no longer feel right. But every shoe must carry its load.

My God knows the pain you bear. He knows every heart. He is an all-knowing God. Surly He can stop the water from pouring into your shoes, and He can ease the pain you feel.

Remembering both good times and bad, Job said:

When his candle shined upon my head, and when by his light I walked through darkness ...
Job 29:3

The Psalmist David sang:

Though I walk in the midst of trouble, thou wilt revive me: thou shalt stretch forth thine hand against the wrath of mine enemies, and thy right hand shall save me. The LORD will perfect that which concerneth me: thy mercy, O LORD, endureth for ever: forsake not the works of thine own hands.   Psalm 138:7-8

So whatever shoe you may be walking in at the moment, the Lord is there to heal, deliver and set you free.

Why Not a Woman?

So, wear your shoes, and wear them in faith, knowing that God will perfect the things that concern you.

Wear your shoes. Wear them in love and not in anger.

Wear your shoes. Wear them no matter the weight you must carry. God will lighten your load.

Wear your shoes. Wear colorful shoes, for there will come a brighter day.

Wear your shoes, remembering God's promises:

Yea, though I walk through the valley of the shadow of death, I will fear no evil: for thou art with me; thy rod and thy staff they comfort me.   Psalm 23:4

Wear your shoes, for God has said that He will never leave us comfortless, but will send a Comforter to help us walk in our pain.

So put on the whole armor of God:

Put on the whole armour of God, that ye may be able to stand against the wiles of the devil.

You Can't Walk in My Shoes

For we wrestle not against flesh and blood, but against principalities, against powers, against the rulers of the darkness of this world, against spiritual wickedness in high places. Wherefore take unto you the whole armour of God, that ye may be able to withstand in the evil day, and having done all, to stand.

                                        Ephesians 6:11-13

While you are walking, count it all joy:

My brethren, count it all joy when ye fall into divers temptations; knowing this, that the trying of your faith worketh patience. But let patience have her perfect work, that ye may be perfect and entire, wanting nothing.

                                        James 1:2-4

Whatever happens around you, keep on walking by faith:

God is our refuge and strength, a very present help in trouble. Therefore will not we fear, though the earth be removed, and though the mountains be carried into the midst of the sea;

though the waters thereof roar and be troubled, though the mountains shake with the swelling thereof. Selah. There is a river, the streams whereof shall make glad the city of God, the holy place of the tabernacles of the most High. God is in the midst of her; she shall not be moved: God shall help her, and that right early.   Psalm 46:1-5

Even when there are wars and rumours of wars, walk on.

Be still, and know that I am God: I will be exalted among the heathen, I will be exalted in the earth.   Psalm 46:10

So I say to you today through this book, "Walk on in Jesus' name!"
WHY NOT A WOMAN?
AND WHY NOT YOU?

Chapter 21

I Am What God Says I Am

And ye shall be unto me a kingdom of priests, and an holy nation. These are the words which thou shalt speak unto the children of Israel.

Exodus 19:6

But ye are a chosen generation, a royal priesthood, an holy nation, a peculiar people; that ye should shew forth the praises of him who hath called you out of darkness into his marvelous light.   1 Peter 2:9

I am part of a royal priesthood. I am here to serve, to function for God. I am set aside for His special service. I have been called out for such a time as this, to be part of a holy nation, a kingdom of priests. I am part of a chosen generation. I am God's own. Therefore I am what He says I am. I had to be delivered out of something, to be brought into His marvelous light. What a great privilege!

You, too, are called out as a peculiar people, and that's why you can't just fit in any old place. The atmosphere in many places makes you feel uncomfortable. You have to be in a place where you can show forth the praises of your God.

You have a shout in you that has to come out. You have a praise on your lips that causes you to sing forth His glorious praise.

You and I are not like other people. We are going forth in God's marvelous light with joy in our hearts, just enjoying His pleasures and the prosperity He brings.

Isaiah 43:4 tells me that I am precious in His sight because He loves me. Psalm 30:4 identifies me as one of His saints. Psalm 89:5 goes further, showing that I am one of His congregation. Deuteronomy 32:10 speaks of me as the apple of His eye. In the Song of Songs, I am His fair love. Psalm 139:14 tells me that *"I am fearfully and wonderful made."*

Oh, yes, I am going to be who God says I am, I am going to go where God wants me to go, and I am going to obey what God tells me to do, for I am an ambassador for Christ.

You and I have been sent out to represent a treaty in Christ, to tell sinners to be reconciled to God, to tell them to believe and to accept His atonement. Yes, I am what God says I am. How about you?

WHY NOT A WOMAN?
AND WHY NOT YOU?

Chapter 22

Jesus, Lover of My Soul

For God so loved the world, that he gave his only begotten Son, that whosoever believeth in him should not perish, but have everlasting life.   John 3:16

We should remind ourselves often of this truth. God loved the whole world, not just men, and not just one type of people, not, for instance, just the rich or the white. Look at yourself and know that God loves you in whatever state you are in.

God loved us all so much that He gave something very dear to Him to redeem us. He designed us and put every element in just the right place. He even made us in His own image. So, no matter how other people view you or how any particular person may perceive you, you are wonderful and fearfully made. Man may take my life, but God wants my soul and spirit.

Jesus, Lover of My Soul

When Jesus went to the cross, having been beaten, and then bled and died, with blood streaming down His broken body, it was for you and me. He bore everything that we face on a daily basis. As He made the ultimate sacrifice, He had you and me on His mind. And now He is seated at the right hand of the Father making intercession for us.

When we read the whole Bible, we see that it is actually a love letter to us from Genesis to Revelation, and it lets us know just how great and how powerful God's love for us is. Sometimes, when you are feeling lonely or tired, sick, depressed or oppressed, the Father wants you to draw nearer to Him because there is the relationship between the Bridegroom and His Bride. When the Father says, "Come," He will take us in His arm and comfort us, gently guide us and keeping us from harm.

He said:

My beloved is mine, and I am his.

Song of Songs 2:16

Why Not a Woman?

He is the Rose of Sharon, and Lily of the Valley (see SOS 2:1), and His banner over me is love (see SOS 2:4).

When the children of Israel had left Egypt, God gave Moses the Ten Commandments. But in Moses' absence, the people had made and were worshiping another god. Moses was so angry that he broke the tablets of stone. He could not understand why the people were so stiffed-necked and why they had sinned so against the God who loved them. Then Moses went back to God:

> *Moses returned unto the LORD and said, Oh this people have sinned, a great sin and have made them gods of gold, yet now if thou will forgive their sin, and if not blot me I pray out of thy book which thou has written.*
>
> Exodus 32:31-32

Think about that! Moses loved these people so much that in spite of his anger against them for their sin, he was willing to die in their place. That love he felt had to come from God. Only God loves in that way.

God did not wipe the Israelites off the fact of the earth, as they deserved. Instead, He loved them so much that He again appeared to Moses, this time in the wilderness Tabernacle the people had built.

The pillar of cloud, symbol of God's presence, descended and stood at the door of the Tabernacle and the Lord talked with Moses. Let God minster to your heart and soul today. Just as He was with Moses, so He will be with you. It is still His desire to commune with His children.

Why not start to sing a sweet song to the Lord, right now, asking Him to come and reveal Himself to you? I guarantee that He wants to talk with you today just as He did with Moses. God's grace extended to Moses is this day extended to you!

WHY NOT A WOMAN?
AND WHY NOT YOU?

Chapter 23

Trust Him

Trust in the LORD with all thine heart; and lean not unto thine own understanding. In all thy ways acknowledge him, and he shall direct thy paths. Proverbs 3:5-6

Too often we let our understanding get in the way, as we try to help God out. When we do this, He just sits back watching to see how far we can go on our own. He knows everything. If you will trust Him, your harvest is right around the corner. The problem is that you are in the way. So, let go and let God.

The prophet Micah said:

Trust ye not in a friend, put ye not confidence in a guide. Micah 7:5

We can't even trust those who call themselves our friends? Why? Because sometimes that person, even the one closet to you, might betray you or deceive you.

People are not perfect. Sometimes, even when they don't mean to hurt you or let you down, their flesh prevails. For this same reason, God has told us to forgive those who offend us, even if it is many times a day. The enemy will use the people around you to try to stop your blessing.

Paul wrote to Timothy:

Charge them that are rich in this world, that they be not highminded, nor trust in uncertain riches, but in the living God, who giveth us richly all things to enjoy. 1 Timothy 6:17

In this passage, God is speaking to believers and warning them not to be proud, for pride can make you do foolish things. God is our Source, so He deserves all praise, not us.

This is important because it is time for your harvest. This your season to be blessed.

The Bible character named Job was very rich, but then one day he suddenly lost everything. Surprisingly, he said:

Why Not a Woman?

Though he [God] slay me, yet will I trust in him: but I will maintain mine own ways before him. Job 13:15

The Bible shows that Job maintained his integrity before God.

If you and I were to lose everything we have, could we still trust God? Or would we blame Him or some other person?

We seem to have a blaming problem, and we need to trust God, get things right with Him and be able to say of a certainty, "Lord, I trust You!"

Trusting God means that you totally release everything from your hand into His, believing that He is able to take care of anything and everything you might face.

In order to trust God, first you must believe that He wants to give you what you are in need of, and secondly, you must have the faith that He will indeed perform it. Didn't He say:

And all things, whatsoever ye shall ask in prayer, believing, ye shall receive. Matthew 21:22

Trust Him

If ye shall ask any thing in my name, I will do it.   John 14:14

As noted, He promised in Matthew 11:28:

Come unto me, all ye that labour and are heavy laden, and I will give you rest.

If you trust Him, this is your season.

In this season, you must think less of self. God has called us to forsake selfishness and walk as Jesus walked, concentrating on the needs of others. While you are out there helping others, God will be ushering in your season.

Are you trusting God for your home and family, husband or wife, children and other family members, your finances and you church? Are you believing for healing and health? Then make sure you are blessing those who misuse you, hate you and speak evil against you.

Abraham trusted God and had the faith to believe Him, and look at what God did for him.

Think about that man who was waiting so long at the Pool of Bethesda for the moving of the water, so that he could get in and be healed. For such a long time, nothing seemed to happen (because it was not his time). But when the right season came, and he got into the pool, he was healed. In the meantime, he didn't give up. He waited patiently for his blessing.

You and I need to trust God more and keep the mind of Christ. This is not a time to give up or turn back because you season of harvest is here.

Trust God with your thoughts, and let your thoughts be toward Him. Think on the things that are good, things that are lovely, things that are of a good report. Then your success will be guaranteed.

Trust God for direction, and let Him direct your paths, so when the fiery darts are thrown at you and Satan comes to buffet you in other ways, you can stand firm and raise up a standard against him, just as Job did.

There is someone I am directing this to right now. Your faith has been low, and you have not been able to trust God as you ought. It's your time, your season.

WHY NOT A WOMAN?
AND WHY NOT YOU?

Be Unstoppable

Women, there will be opposition
that will come in your life.
There will be changes that come.
There will be hurts and disappointments.
But be unstoppable.
If there is a goal you are working toward,
know that God is in there with you,
to help you.
Esther said, "If I perish, I perish!"
If God has put something in your
heart, and it seems too hard
and looks like it's not going to happen,
make the determination in your heart:
"I must press on!"
This is not the time for giving up.
When we look at the Proverbs 31 woman,
she showed a tremendous amount of strength.
She pressed in every way
for her husband,
her children
and everything else she had to do.

Chapter 24

God Will Withhold No Good Thing from You

Bring ye all the tithes into the storehouse, that there may be meat in mine house, and prove me now herewith, saith the LORD of hosts, if I will not open you the windows of heaven, and pour you out a blessing, that there shall not be room enough to receive it. And I will rebuke the devourer for your sakes, and he shall not destroy the fruits of your ground; neither shall your vine cast her fruit before the time in the field, saith the LORD *of hosts.*   Malachi 3:10-11

God loves you so much, and His mercies are new to you every morning. So, why can't this be your season? This is what I am hearing in the Spirit. Please hear what the Spirit has to say to the churches (and to you personally) today.

God has said to you, *"I will OPEN the windows of heaven and POUR out a blessing on*

148

you that there shall not be room to receive it." That is for you. God wants you to believe Him for your season of harvest.

God says that because we are faithful with our tithes, He will prosper us. He is ready and able to bless you in this season.

God said, *"I will rebuke the devourer."* I don't care what's eating at you, if this is your season, God is ready to stop it from destroying your blessing.

God promised to CRIPPLE and PARALYZE the enemy so that he would not come near you (see Psalm 91:10). Receive your promise!

God said He would not allow the enemy to destroy the fruit of your ground. Stand on that promise. God said that because of you obedience to Him, He would not allow the enemy to touch your finances, which is the fruit of your ground. You can even ask God not to let the vine cast its fruit before its time.

You need to let your faith build and know that God has just showed His love to you in seven different ways. Seven stands for completion, and we are complete in God.

Therefore the enemy cannot touch my family, my finances, my fruit or my ground, because God said He would give me the ground I walk on.

There is nothing slack about God concerning His promises (see 2 Peter 3:9). He just want us to have the faith and trust Him, Who is the Author and the Finisher of all things. There is nothing He doesn't know and nothing He cannot do, because He is all-knowing and all-powerful to accomplish all things.

God's promise of blessing didn't start in Malachi. It can be found in His Word from the beginning to the end. It is His good will to bless you today.

Blessed shalt thou be in the city, and blessed shalt thou be in the field.

Deuteronomy 28:3

WHY NOT A WOMAN?
AND WHY NOT YOU?

Genesis 1:26

I am made in His image.
I am made after His likeness.
I am held by the three persons
of the divine Trinity,
Father, Son and Holy Ghost.
Since I am made in His likeness,
that enables me to have fellowship with Him.

In His image, God created man.
The image of God was then lost at the Fall.
The restoration of His image was carried
out at the cross.
But the completion of that restoration
will not take place until the
First Resurrection.

Chapter 25

Your Are a Chosen Vessel

But the Lord said unto him, Go thy way: for he is a chosen vessel unto me, to bear my name before the Gentiles, and kings, and the children of Israel. Acts 9:15

Now that you have finished reading this book, tell me: have you not wondered, *Why not me?* Then go into your secret closet, begin to pray and just ask God to show you why.

God said that Paul was a *"chosen vessel,"* chosen to bear His name before the Gentiles, kings and the children of Israel. And, in the very same way, you are also a chosen vessel. God chose you before the foundation of the world, and He alone knows your true purpose, your true reason for living.

A vessel is a container, and it carries or holds something precious and valuable. Think about the woman of Luke 7:36-39. The

Your Are a Chosen Vessel

Bible shows that she was a sinner, but she had a small alabaster box (just big enough to fit her hands) with precious oil in it. You are like that container that held something important inside. Inside of you are the fruits of the Spirit. You just need to practice them and walk in them. Then you will realize that God's love covers a multitudes of sins, like it did with the woman with the oil or like it did with the woman Jesus met at the well of Samaria.

Jesus told this woman that she'd had five husbands and that the man she was even then living with was not her husband. And yet He extended to her the living water that only He could give. To a woman taken in the very act of adultery, a woman who should have been stoned to death according to the Law, He said:

Neither do I condemn thee: go, and sin no more. John 8:1

God's not looking for perfect people, just willing vessels. If a vessel bears Jesus' name and His power, power that can remove every doubt, cast out every oppressive spirit and cause men and women to rise up and stand for righteousness, that's all that matters.

Because of the powerful blood of the Lamb, I am not afraid to stand before presidents, governors, mayors or any other great person and say, "I have been redeemed! God says that I am in Him, and He is in me!" And that's the most important thing in life.

Our God has said:

Cry aloud, spare not, lift up thy voice like a trumpet, and shew my people their transgression, and the house of Jacob their sins. Isaiah 58:1

O highly favored one, as I write this last chapter, it is 2:30 in the morning and the lighting is flashing and the thunder is rolling outside. But on the inside of me the Holy Spirit is moving on my inner man, telling me to encourage every one of you women that there is something on the inside of you, as you step out, as you walk and as you yield yourself to the Holy Spirit. You need to know what's on the inside of you so that you can walk in your full potential. David sang:

Deep calleth unto deep. Psalm 42:7

So, now, arise from your sleep, awake from your slumber, for your light has come. God is ready to empower you, to strengthen you where you have been weak and to encourage you where you have lost hope because of the difficult circumstances of life. I was always taught never to say never, because it is the Lord's will for each of us to prosper and to be used by Him for His glory in this world.

Why don't you take time right now to thank God. We cannot thank Him enough. Your thankfulness will help bring forth what's already inside of you. You will begin to recognize who you really are and begin to see a different direction for your life.

Things won't always remain the same old way they have been until now. You have been created to make a difference in someone's life, and now God is giving you another chance to walk in your purpose, the great destiny that is set before you. I pray you Godspeed on your journey!

WHY NOT A WOMAN?
AND WHY NOT YOU?

Author Contact Page

You may contact the author in the following ways:

Pastor Evangelist Vivian Collins
P.O. Box 1704
Marrero, LA 70073

Phone: 504-347-5797

Tune in to her weekly radio program heard every Sunday night at 7 pm Central time, by dialing 1-714-409-0578 on your telephone or via Facebook or Twitter.

www.ingramcontent.com/pod-product-compliance
Lightning Source LLC
LaVergne TN
LVHW011201080426
835508LV00007B/535